Splish Splash

by Christie Holmgren

This book is dedicated to my grandchildren who inspire me every day.

Copyright ©2017 Christie Holmgren

All photos by Christie Holmgren. All rights reserved. Reproduction by any means—graphic, electronic, or mechanical—of the whole or any part of the contents of this book is prohibited without the prior written permission of the author/photographer.

First Printing 2017

ISBN-13: 978-0692937426
ISBN-10: 0692937420

Library of Congress Control Number: 2017912909

Published by Life's so Sweet
Portland, Oregon

www.life-so-sweet.com

Ordering Information:

U.S. bookstores and wholesalers, please contact:
information@life-so-sweet.com

Splish splash, Mr. Towhee takes a bath.

He wiggles and he wags, making sure the water is just right.

Water goes everywhere, but he doesn't care.

His mother isn't around to tell him not to make a mess.

It looks like a goldfinch wants to join in the fun.

"Too bad," says the towhee. "This tub is taken. Go find your own."

And so she does.

Splish splash, her friends join the bath.

"Last one in is a rotten egg!"

A house finch and pine siskins stop for a drink.

Oh, oh, the starlings arrive and all the fun's over while they take a dive.

"Time to dry off," says the towhee.

"Not so fast," says Ms. Robin. I want a nice bath."

"Ooh, this *is* nice."

Splish splash. She really gets into it!

Wiggle, waggle, shake, shake.

"I guess that's enough for now."

But wait, who's this?

A common yellowthroat takes her turn.

"What's all the commotion about?" ask the cedar waxwings.

"We want to play in the water, too."

Splish splash, wiggle, thrash...

"This sure is refreshing on a hot day!"

An English sparrow wants to cool off.

She patiently awaits her turn.

"I'll try this bath instead."

Splish splash!

"Welcome, my friends."

The cedar waxwings and a goldfinch come to check it out.

But the male English sparrow isn't quite so friendly.

"I'm parched," says the song sparrow.

"Ah, a cool drink of water is just the ticket."

A Western tanager eyes the water.

He's not so sure he will like it.

But he decides to give it a try.

He dips his head.

Now he's all in.

Splish splash!

"Wow, I really like this bath."

"I might try this again sometime."

A young scrub jay comes to bathe.

Wiggle, wag, splish, splash.

Looks like bathtime's over for our feathered friends.

Now it's your turn to take a bath. Won't it be fun!

www.ingramcontent.com/pod-product-compliance
Lightning Source LLC
LaVergne TN
LVHW071027070426
835507LV00002B/50